Frank Horvat
Virtual Zoo

Frank Horvat
Virtual Zoo

Text by Daniele Brolli

Smithsonian Institution Press
Washington, D.C.

© 1995 by Federico Motta Editore, Milan
© 1995 by Frank Horvat for the photographs
© 1998 by the Smithsonian Institution for the
English text
All rights reserved

Published 1998 in the United States of America
by Smithsonian Institution Press
in association with Federico Motta Editore, Milan

Translation from Italian by Renata Treitel

04 03 02 01 00 99 98   5 4 3 2 1

Printed by Arti Grafiche Motta, Milan
Manufactured in Italy, not at government expense

Library of Congress Cataloging-in-Publication Data

Horvat, Frank.   1928–
   [Bestiario virtuale. English]
   Virtual zoo / Frank Horvat ; text by Daniele
Brolli.
      p.   cm.
   Originally published in Italian in 1995 by
Federico Motta Editore of Milan
   Translation of: Bestiario virtuale.
   ISBN 1-56098-443-0 (cloth : alk. paper)
   1. Photography of animals.   2. Virtual reality.
3. Horvat, Frank, 1928–   .   I. Brolli, Daniele,
1959–   .   II. Title.   III. Series.
TR727.H671998
779′.32—dc21   98-4158

Virtual Zoo

In the large house of memories the cabinet of the dish drainer above the sink hangs crookedly and its doors are painted in white enamel. It sticks forward because the wall hooks that hold it up have pushed their way through the wall and have the illusion of slipping away from it just as the decals, higgledy-piggledy on their surface, are home there. It is a question of threatening doors. They creak on hinges that are almost rusty and, on their sharp edges that are peeling off, one can study the geo-logical eras of the enamel coats. Each decal on it has the right of citizenship. And silhouetted on the white screen of the imaginary, the figures of the animals free themselves from the stylized representation.

A zoo borrowed from the diorama of a museum of natural history whirls and threatens the observing child. There is a bear that seems to feel perfectly at ease on the expanse the color of ice. An elephant trumpets in the immense savanna bereft of a horizon. A rolled-up snake rests under a blinding sun that overexposes the rocks. The fawn hobbles dangerously on the heap of stones. As soon as it is seen, each of the animals represented is placed again in its imaginary territory, freed from the two-dimensional frame and restored to a mythic ecosystem gazed at in a school textbook or on a TV program. Light glides, lives uncertainly in the areas where the underlying dampness and colors ooze up. They are perspective splashes in which the eye loses certainty of vision and catches glimpses of fantastic territories in which the animals will move more at ease than in their own ecosystem. The unconscious seems to know without a shade of doubt that the natural context does not favor the well-being of the subject: perhaps it flatters it with smells and flavors, with the vigor of power, but ultimately it aims at making of him nothing else but suffering food and manure. The difference between man and the other living beings of the earth is really the following: man's stubborn and often vain organizing of bold escapes from the natural cages with the purpose of improving his own life conditions: escapes that instead, often with Byzantine twists, end up taking him back to the ties of origin. It is difficult to cast aside in a few centuries the traps that a process of millions of years has painstakingly set up. One would need a brand-new universe.

Photography contains the solitude of the eye with the kingdom of its fantasies. The world recomposes itself thanks to the whim or the reasoning of the photographer (whoever he is, professional or amateur) with a sometimes unconscious design in the glance. It has to do with discreet modifications, made without violating the substance of things. The variables that determine them can be aesthetic or born from production motivations (in one of the various commercial centers with whom photography has relationships: book trade, fashion, industry, medicine, publicity and its various sectors . . .). But it is always the exoticism of the moment that invents the world in the image of and resemblance to the eye, naïve by definition, that sees things being born in the same moment in which, by means of the ritual of the click, they make an impression on the film. Let us now cast aside the practical ends of photography, the use and motivations by which the greatest number of photographs are produced. It is true that a hypothetical visitor from the stars descending to our planet after a selective holocaust that would leave untouched only a few (or many, or all) of the photographic images would get an idea of the history of civilization very far from reality, without mentioning the paradoxes of some promotional still-lifes, monstrous or not, or the compositional abstractions of the body in fashion photos. Even if he examined only reproductions of a photoreport, he would compose a very strange vision of the world: bodies balanced on strange centers of gravity and an expressiveness always liminal, at the boundary between the forbidden and the permitted, mannequins at the edge of time and death. The specific infancy of the photographic instant (which, different from that of a film frame, is not limited by any sequential duty) plays with the dimensional appearance of things decontextualizing and recontextualizing them, declaring the circumstance of the perceiving intuition absolute. Everything that objectifies life is cast aside in favor of the essential interpretation of the subject (whether it is the photographer or observer). The concept of experience seeks shelter in the "I" and transforms itself in a filter of perception and *testimonial*, that is to say, partial view, subjected to the continuous disavowals of the multiplying of testimonials and to the deceits of the points of view, alien to the dominant variables of the real: space and time. Reality in photography, even if not explicitly admitted, is *virtual* by definition.

Perhaps this essential contradiction makes photography a consoling medium because, while playing a role of carrying over in the process of formation of the social imagination, it ends up despite itself speaking about the past without saying anything at all about the future. But probably the encounter with the new information technologies capable of making the universe of the images absolute, rendering it into an autonomous cosmos, with new spatial-temporal dynamics, can enable it to overcome this *impasse*. To organize dreams, in other words, to be carriers of a possibility of metaphysical chatter cast beyond the pain of being, through the decomposition of the ideas and their recombination into a particular vision, is the prerogative of a hypothetical universe in the process of formation. The dimension of the new electronic technologies operates truly according to this possibility, opening up endless new territories that are linked to the strength and substance of thought. It is a mistake to think that photography can enter the vast immaterial field of virtual realities entrusting itself to the crass evidence of the synthetic image. Photography is an instrument that long ago overcame its pioneering phase to move away from explorative dynamics of experimentation of the medium and has developed a language so complex that it can appear chaotic to the hypothetical extraterrestrial visitor but, more simply, is just art for us. On the other hand, the real virtual realities are a sensorial prosthesis, an often liberating extension of the body that exalts the desiring vortex of the imaginary. Through them, we can go beyond the physical limits of time and space and can structure universes which, according to the circumstances, respond to our fantasies or to one of the possible practical exploitations of *virtual realities* that condenses mainly in the field of telepresence (that is to say, where the human presence, for either logistical reasons or for warding off risk factors, is substituted by a precision camera guided by a system of *feedback* that has the sensorial impulses of the photographer).

In considering the utilization of the synthetic image in photography, Frank Horvat has avoided the sensationalist factor of artificial appearance. He has favored instead the form of technological extension that the computer can represent. On their own, our eyes are unable to transmit to our brain the image of what surrounds us. The light that reaches the retina is only part of the one that enters into the pupil, and insufficient elements reach our brain to define by themselves the object of vision. But the neurobiological mechanism of vision is such that the brain recognizes the signs that are provided and reconstitutes the entire image on the basis of its interpretation. What we see (or *believe* we see) is the product of a mediation between our eyes in their sensorial function and our brain as a processor of images. This mechanism is totally analogous to the system of virtual realities, in which our brain recognizes by illusion, through the sensorial *input* programmed by a computer, scenes and situations produced in the ambit of synthesis of digital images. What gets exploited is the principle of feedback in which man's mind is also capable of reconstructing entire segments missing from reality if only to present an illusion of continuity that sustains a psychological stabilization. In their experimental

VII

function and in their function of electronic games, these artificial contexts invent fantastic universes used for adventurous and extraordinary activities of which the sensation of flight is by now the simplest one. But they are also used to reconstitute real situations simulated with preset variables with the purpose of training or instructing. One of the real handicaps of virtual reality is perhaps the one that gives the sensation that, with adequate electronic planning, everything can be possible and any fantasy feasible. It is true that in these scenes the body experiences the electronic ecstasy of acting and thinking in a space and in a time not yet determined and, above all, the capacity of being able to set the rules and glide from one context to another at will according to the circumstances, with a speed that makes everything immediate, definable in *real time.* It creates a sensation of power capable of hallucinatory effects. It also takes the conscience of self to the edge of drowning with an ecstasy bereft of mystical coordinates, a sensorial excitement which stimulates the cognitive processes and speeds up the learning process. Through virtual reality an alternative universe is born (in which it is fundamental the awareness that, in each case, we are not dealing with a substitute cosmos) in which body and mind can live a Promethean-like life of which they are creators who have it in their power to plan its coordinates. This parallel existence always bespeaks the real one, experimentally or implicitly, becoming an instrument to probe its dynamics in depth.

The use Horvat makes in his bestiary of the virtual potentials of photographs filtered through an encounter with the new technologies has the discreet measure of an analytic journey into the recesses of the electronic mind. Horvat has photographed a series of animals in captivity and has returned them to a natural setting by means of electronic insertion. But the background of these photos is not the animals' original ecosystem, it is something that resembles it. Or, rather, it appears like a plausible simulation of what might appear to an observer to be the ambiance of reference of the photographed animals. The African elephant and the zebra in California, the Asian rhinoceros and the lion in New Mexico, the tiger in France and the crocodile in the waters of the Loire. . . . Horvat works on the cognitive processes of the observer's mind. These processes complete the picture of the image, perfecting the mode of electronic fusion of the subject with its background. Each of these photos, deprived of an explicit declaration like the title *Virtual Zoo,* could live at ease in the deception of the successful simulation. It would be a "perfect crime." A false consolation about zoo animals which are difficult to imagine in a natural state. But it would be reductive to think of the photographs in *Virtual Zoo* as confined to an ecological intention which, even while being hypothetical, represents only a complication of a broader discourse. In declaring his game, Horvat raises the curtain on the possibility of a conspiracy plotted with the involuntary complicity of our own cognitive processes. How much do our observations and our brain complete the information we receive daily, making it not only plausible but also acceptable, insertable in the reassuring context of normalcy? What would happen if we suddenly rejected our terrestrial citizenship in order to declare ourselves alien and evaluated all types of solicitations we receive from the world of information?

All things may appear arranged, disguised, ordered by a god in view of unquestionable ends. Let us imagine then the dream of an idiot god (the idiot god of science): an endless diorama where everything is under control, where each thing has the ability to interact with another. Everything is reproducible, everything is convertible, everything can be assigned to a place and each place is right because there exists only one choice which cannot be questioned except for errors of operation. But this god that knows no limits, that is both infamous and muddle-headed, bestows only pain on his creatures. Horvat's photos could be read also this way, as a metaphor of man's intoxication with omnipotence face-to-face with the possibility acquired by means of computer science to manipulate the idea of a natural universe which, in its substance, is already on a collision course with its own working rules, and returning to it a precarious imaginary balance.

Victor Segalen wrote in his *Saggio sull'esotismo* (Bologna 1983) that "the external world is that which differentiates itself immediately from us. . . . the sentiment for nature has only existed from the moment in which man was able to conceive it as different from himself." In his notes accompanying the idea of journey, not only through unknown continents but above all in the interior of our vision of things, Segalen has written a recipe for the disease which afflicts desires. The knot lies in being able to see in a different manner, to intuit the singleness and the divergence of visions, their appearance, at bottom chaotic, and admit that their right to exist does not belong to an abstract concept of justice, but is a patrimony of an ethics that regulates the possibility of the universe to exist.

One can presume that Frank Horvat's zoo also contains in an ambivalent way, though coherent in its significance, this hypothesis of individuality in the vision of things (which are such only in the point of view of the perceiver). On the other hand, the hypothesis is symmetrical to the denunciation of their conformity, from which it is separated by the thin membrane of the awareness of the glance, and invites us once again to look beyond the reassuring certainties in order to discover that only doubts give substance again to the world.

Daniele Brolli
Translated from the Italian by Renata Treitel

Images

31